5S Made Easy

A Step-by-Step Guide to Implementing and Sustaining Your 5S Program

David Visco

CRC Press
Taylor & Francis Group
Boca Raton   London   New York

CRC Press is an imprint of the
Taylor & Francis Group, an **informa** business

A PRODUCTIVITY PRESS BOOK

CRC Press
Taylor & Francis Group
6000 Broken Sound Parkway NW, Suite 300
Boca Raton, FL 33487-2742

© 2016 by Taylor & Francis Group, LLC
CRC Press is an imprint of Taylor & Francis Group, an Informa business

No claim to original U.S. Government works

Printed on acid-free paper
Version Date: 20150721

International Standard Book Number-13: 978-1-4987-1982-7 (Paperback)

**Visit the Taylor & Francis Web site at
http://www.taylorandfrancis.com**

**and the CRC Press Web site at
http://www.crcpress.com**

Contents

Foreword

5S has become one of the most popular improvement activities in factories, offices, and small shops across America. 5S is straightforward and effective in improving any operation.

Despite its popularity, there are only a handful of books that explain how to do 5S. Veteran 5S coach and consultant David Visco has stepped in to help fill that gap with his "how-to" workbook, *5S Made Easy*. Anyone can begin a 5S program in their department or business by following this book's easy-to-understand steps. In addition, Visco has provided checklists, forms, and resource guides. Almost everything you need is right here. And, he shows you where to get the materials you need.

In that sense, Visco has "5S-ed" the process of implementing 5S: simple, understandable steps; checklists of what to do; checklists of materials you will need, and where to get them. Truly, *5S Made Easy*.

So, what are you waiting for? David Visco has made 5S easy for you. Get started!

Mike McCarthy
Lean Consultant
Author of *Sustain Your Gains: The People Side of Lean–Six Sigma*

Preface

Why I Wrote This Book

I first learned about 5S over a decade ago, while working for a global medical device manufacturer in Massachusetts. I had always been known as an organized guy and the department I managed with my team was impeccable—a thing of beauty. Or so I thought. When I learned about the opportunities for additional improvement that 5S could bring us, I was hooked. I read several books (blogs were not really a thing quite yet) and Google was just starting to explode. The information available at the time was somewhat limited. Finding supplies, well, that is a whole other topic altogether.

Ever since then I have been studying, learning, implementing, failing, succeeding, failing, and trying again at 5S until I finally figured out the best methodologies needed for a successful 5S program. There are some good books out there on the topic but *none* are laid out like the book you hold in your hands.

I have taken all my learning, research, and success from the last decade and compiled it into this one of a kind, easy-to-follow, step-by-step workbook. I am confident that if you follow the steps as they are laid out, you will find 5S has been *made easy* for you.

Tell me your story! E-mail your successes, failures, and lessons learned to me at: David.Visco@the5Sstore.com. While I cannot promise to use your specific story, I will be selecting stories and lessons learned for my next book, *True Stories of 5S Made Easy*. If your story is selected, you will be listed in the acknowledgments and receive a complimentary copy.

David Visco
5S Expert

Chapter 1

What Is 5S and Why Do It?

What Is 5S?

5S at its core is about removing non-value-added processes by developing standard methods for doing the necessary work. An effective 5S program therefore improves efficiency, quality, workflow, and employee safety.

5S is based on the Japanese words that begin with the letter "s."

- Sort (*Seiri*)
- Set in Order (*Seiton*)
- Shine (*Seiso*)
- Standardize (*Seiketsu*)
- Sustain (*Shitsuke*)

These five "pillars" make up the 5S System (as seen in Figure 1.1).

Benefits of 5S

- Saves time wasted searching for tools.
- Reduces the amount of walking to complete tasks.
- Increases safety by eliminating stretching, bending, and tripping hazards.
- Increases equipment reliability.
- Standardizes steps for easier and more accurate cross-training.
- Frees up valuable floor space.
- Helps lay the foundation for a continuous improvement culture.

Summary of Each of the 5 Pillars

Sort—Sort is the process of removing everything that is not needed in the area. This process involves going into every nook and cranny of the area,

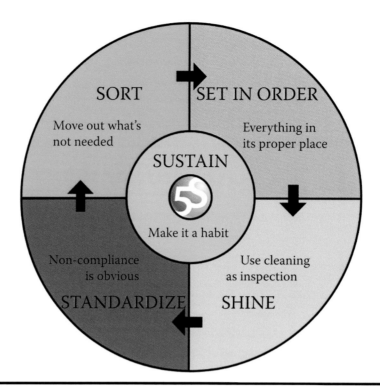

Figure 1.1 5S Circle

all drawers, cabinets, shelves, corners, and closets. This is addressed during a red tag event when people walk through the area with pre-made red tags (either adhesive or wired) and label anything they deem unnecessary in the area. All red-tagged items are then moved to the predetermined red tag area for future disposition.

Set in Order—Is basically the process of laying out tools, equipment, and processes at the point of use for the worker while also improving overall safety and ergonomics. This step typically takes longer than the others and requires a number of 5S materials such as floor tape, tool control foam, pegboards, tool shadow tape, label machines, and much more.

Shine—Much of this step is handled during the Set in Order step. The intent here is threefold. First, clean the area, which may include scrubbing or painting equipment, replacing floors, painting walls, and more. Second, develop a schedule and responsibilities to make sure the area is kept up to standards. Third, and most important, Shine provides an atmosphere where we are able to use cleaning as a way of inspecting equipment by making it easier to spot machinery in need of repair (for example, oil leaks are more noticeable in a clean environment).

Standardize—This step helps set clear, visible methods for how the agreed upon status of the area should be kept. One of the key tools used for standardizing is the 5S Audit. Audits are routinely conducted based on a strict set of standards. These audit results are posted and monitored. Necessary actions taken to improve the results are noted.

Sustain—Considered to be the most difficult of the 5 pillars, Sustain is the routine that keeps everything from going back to the way it was before 5S. This is actually much easier than most think. Sustain just takes repetition, diligence, and accountability until it becomes a habit.

How Is It Implemented?

This outline is just a summary. We will go in depth on implementing each of the 5 pillars in the forthcoming chapters. The pillars are generally implemented in order with one pillar following after the other.

Once a company decides to move forward with 5S, it is important to plan appropriately. Some items to consider are choosing the right project leader, 5S champion, team members, the size of the area to address, timeframe, and ultimate goal.

Project Leader—It is important that the project leader is someone who has a thorough understanding of 5S and significant experience managing and implementing process change.

5S Champion—This is typically the person responsible for the area. They will be in the trenches while also giving guidance and instruction to the team.

Team Members—Make sure to get everyone that works directly in the area involved with the 5S implementation. Additionally, it is a good idea to have one or two people from outside the department, for some "fresh eyes" on the situation.

Size of the Area—Some companies opt to implement 5S across the entire plant all at once. This is generally a bad idea. It is much more effective to choose an area around 1000 sq. ft. so that all of the necessary work can be completed. Ideally, choose an area where a set of work processes begin and end. 5S should help the work to flow through this set of processes.

Timeframe—There are two options with regard to the timeframe for the initial 5S event. Option 1 is to close down the area for 3 to 4 days and have the team dedicated to this event. Option 2 is to roll it out for a few hours a week or one day a week until the event is complete. Many companies find this option easier to manage, as it is less disruptive to the operation.

Ultimate Goal—As with any process change, it is important to determine the overall objective before proceeding. Some companies use the first three pillars, Sort, Set in Order, and Shine to simply clean up the place. While this gets the area cleaned up, it will not be sustainable without the other two pillars, Standardize and Sustain. The company needs to decide upfront whether this is just a quick cleanup project or an overall change on how to manage their work process. A true 5S program never ends, as it is always making the workflow easier, safer, and faster.

Action Items

1. _____
2. _____
3. _____
4. _____
5. _____
6. _____

Parking Lot Items

Ideas and issues out of scope but still worth capturing:

1. _____
2. _____
3. _____
4. _____
5. _____
6. _____

Chapter 2

How to Use This Book

There are many books available on the subject of 5S. While some of them are good on content, they all fail at providing an implementation plan that is easy to follow—until now. In *5S Made Easy* we have provided you with an easy-to-use, systematic, step-by-step workbook for implementing a successful 5S program that is effective and sustainable.

This book is written for the project leader and the team members responsible for implementing the 5S program in the area.

For the process to be effective, you must follow the book in the order it is presented. Do not skip right to Set in Order to clean up your workspace. If you are just looking for some ideas on ways to prepare an area for an upcoming tour, I suppose you could focus on Chapter 6: "Set in Order and Shine." But trust me, all the hard work will disappear within a few short days or weeks along with all of the goodwill and positive feelings generated during the cleanup.

If, however, you are serious about finally learning how to implement a 5S program that will help your production and be sustained over the long term, follow the book in order. Do the steps as suggested. Do not skip a thing. The guidance in this book is built on over a decade of proven methodologies and hands-on experience from the author. 5S is a system that will not function properly without all of the pieces. Similar to a house of cards, remove one card and the house just might hold, but remove just one more card and you will likely have a mess on your hands.

I suggest that you create a 2-inch three-ring binder to keep all of your 5S documents to use in the future as a reference guide. All documents and worksheets throughout the book can be downloaded from the *5S Made Easy* category on our website, The 5S Store, at: www.the5Sstore.com/5SMadeEasy.

Ok, now, let's get to work.

Action Items

1. _____
2. _____
3. _____
4. _____
5. _____
6. _____

Parking Lot Items

Ideas and issues out of scope but still worth capturing:

1. _____
2. _____
3. _____
4. _____
5. _____
6. _____

Notes

_____
_____
_____
_____
_____
_____

Chapter 3

Develop Your Plan

Before jumping into your 5S program, it is absolutely critical that you develop a plan. While most of us prefer to not think of 5S as a project, there is still an initial project-like component: planning. Where 5S differs from most projects is that projects have an end date. 5S, for lack of a better term, is a journey with no end date. The initial implementation of the 5S pillars will have an end date. However, there is a routine to establish that will sustain all that has been accomplished. Like brushing your teeth, there are 5S procedures that have to be done as a daily routine.

With that said, let's begin this journey by creating a project plan using the 5S Project Charter form (Figure 3.1). See the "Forms" section at the end of this book, or as with all the forms, go to The 5S Store at: www.the5Sstore.com/5SMadeEasy to download the forms for use.

Step 1: Get a 2-inch three-ring binder to store all of the project documents. Also, if you have access to your company computer server, create a shared folder to store all pictures, documents, action items, parking lot items, and so on.

Step 2: Determine which area to implement 5S. Consider the following: How many shifts are running in this area? It is best to work on an area that has only one shift—if at all possible. If only multiple shifts are available, make sure to keep the other shifts up to date on what is going on and arrange a forum to get their input. Truth be told, managing multiple shifts when implementing 5S can be a challenge because people on the other shifts will not have the same understanding of what is going on as the people implementing 5S.

Caution

Do not lose sight of the need to include these other shifts and inform them of what changes were made and why. Otherwise they might

5S Project Charter

Project Authorization						
Organization:		Coach:			Project Lead:	
Project Title:					Project Area Name:	
What are the challenges?						
Project Objective:						
Target Completion Date:		Estimated Benefits:				
Coach Signature:		Project Lead Signature:			Approval Date:	

Project Team			
Name	Role	E-mail Address	Phone

Scope	
Critical to Customer Satisfaction:	
Inside Scope of Project:	Outside Scope of Project:

Figure 3.1   5S Project Charter

"undo" any rearrangement of the work area. For example, a colleague of mine tells the story of one group moving the machinery to make a smoother production flow, only to find that the 3rd shift had moved it all back overnight. Nobody had informed the 3rd shift of the changes.

Is this area one where you can really make a big splash—a showcase area—a best practice 5S area? Choose your area wisely.

Try and keep the area under 1000 square feet and make it an area or department where a sub-process starts and stops (before handing off the product to another department).

Will you shut down the area for 3 to 4 days and complete the implementation, or will you do the implementation in pieces spread out over several weeks? If you have the slack in your production schedule to do it all at once, then you have the advantage of a quicker and smoother transition. If you cannot shut down, then you need to spread the implementation out over several weeks. Progress will be slower, but you can continue with production. A benefit of spreading the implementation out over several weeks is that people can stay focused on 5S during the training and not worry about the workload that may be building up back at their desk or workstation.

Step 3: Complete the Project Charter. Some tips for creating your 5S Project Charter follow:

Where the charter says "Critical to Customer Satisfaction," make a list of things that cannot be changed because the customer requires them.

Where the charter says "Inside Scope of Project," list two to three examples of things that are okay to change. These are things that your department controls and do not affect the product or other departments, such as where you store your tools.

Where the charter says "Outside Scope of Project," list any things that you are not allowed to change. These are things that may affect product quality, delivery time, or cost. For example, buying a new CNC milling machine. Other out of scope items for most 5S events would be elements that force big changes on departments upstream or downstream of the operation where you are implementing 5S. An example would be deciding that you will work on certain product models only on Mondays.

Step 4: Make a list of the tools and supplies you will need. Order them and stage them in the area you chose for your 5S event.

Caution

Keep in mind that you need to order Set in Order materials prior to your Set in Order event. You should plan on at least a 2-week lead time to receive all of your items. You will find a suggested "5S Materials Checklist" at the end of this book. You can also contact one of the experts at The 5S Store at: www.the5Sstore.com or (978) 842-4610, and tell them you are following the *5S Made Easy* workbook and could use some help determining which products you need. A great idea is to take some pictures of the area and send them to The 5S Store expert and arrange for a free 30-minute consult. The staff are very happy to help you on your way. This preparation and going to an expert first who knows the *5S Made Easy* methodologies can also save you a lot of time and money.

Step 5: Inform all the other departments about your implementation plan. Make it clear that you and your teammates are not to be disturbed during the implementation times.

Tip

Get a "5S in Session" sign (Figure 3.2) and put it in the area when you are in the midst of the event. Make sure everyone understands what this sign means.

Figure 3.2 "5S IN SESSION" Sign Pal (Courtesy of The 5S Store, LLC, Pepperell, MA, and Accuform Signs, Brooksville, FL.)

Caution

The leader of the team absolutely has to set this precedent and lead by example. Stay off your smartphone and laptop during the event and do not let anyone pull you away.

Tip

Contact the facilities department in particular. Ask for their help. This group can prove extremely beneficial if equipment needs to be moved or power needs to be disconnected or sign hanging is required. Keep them in the loop, invite them to lunches, and notify their manager. This level of inclusion will garner respect and the support you need—while also keeping your team safe.

Step 6: Before you begin the Sort process, make sure to take plenty of *before* pictures.

Tip

Try and take the pictures from positions that you can use in the future for your *after* pictures. The "before and after" pictures are more effective if the viewpoints are identical.

Develop Your Plan: Summary of Steps

☐ Get a 2-inch three-ring binder to store all of the project documents.
☐ Determine which area to implement 5S.
☐ Complete the Project Charter.
☐ Make a list of the tools and supplies you need.
☐ Inform all other departments about your implementation plan.
☐ Take plenty of *before* pictures.

Action Items

1. _____
2. _____
3. _____
4. _____
5. _____
6. _____

Parking Lot Items

Ideas and issues out of scope but still worth capturing:

1. _____
2. _____
3. _____
4. _____
5. _____
6. _____

Notes

_____
_____
_____
_____
_____
_____
_____

Chapter 4

Train the Team

It is critical to the success of your 5S program that you properly train the people that will work in the area. Do not rush through this initial training. This will likely be all new jargon and strategies for the group. The unknown scares people and can put them on the defensive. As the leader it is imperative for you to listen with sincere empathy. Additionally, make sure the team understands that most of these steps will require their ideas and hands-on effort from them, not you, and not the Lean manager. This is a team effort. It is up to the team members. It is your responsibility as the leader to make this point abundantly clear, as well as to hold yourself to this standard.

Tip

Have a mind-set that if you were away for several months after the 5S implementation, the area would look even better when you returned because the team and you put in a standardized process (the fourth S) that the team owned and took pride in.

Step 1: Use the *What, Why, Where, When,* and *How* format to explain what 5S is all about:

- *What*—5S at its core is about removing non-value-added processes by developing standard methods (one best way) for doing the daily work. An effective 5S program therefore improves efficiency, quality, and employee safety. All of us will do the work this standard way. 5S is roughly based on the Japanese words that begin with the letter "*s*."
    - Sort (*Seiri*)
    - Set in Order (*Seiton*)
    - Shine (*Seiso*)
    - Standardize (*Seiketsu*)
    - Sustain (*Shitsuke*)

- *Why?* (Benefits)
  - Saves time wasted searching for tools.
  - Reduces the amount of walking to complete tasks.
  - Reduces non-value-added steps thereby improving efficiency.
  - Increases safety by eliminating stretching, bending, and tripping hazards.
  - Increases equipment reliability by making malfunctions easier to spot.
  - Standardizes steps for easier and more accurate cross-training.
  - Frees up valuable floor space.
  - Helps make production flow more smooth and continuous.
- *Where*—The area where the event will take place.
- When—What implementation plan have you chosen? A little bit each week or shut down the area for several days?
- How—Show the project plan. Explain that there will be some classroom style training but that most of the learning will be hands on out on the shop floor. Explain that you will follow a step-by-step format provided by author and 5S expert, David Visco, president of The 5S Store.

Step 2: Go through the PowerPoint presentation found at: www.the5Sstore. com/5SMadeEasy. Schedule 1 hour to go through the slides and make sure to leave plenty of time for Q&A.

Tip

Ask for examples about how you can use the ideas in your area and write them into the "Team Ideas" section at the end of this chapter. Refer back to these ideas during the Set in Order step.

Step 3: Following the PowerPoint slide show, we suggest the team watch a brief video. Studies have shown that learning through a few different methods helps solidify the learning. There are several videos on the market today. We suggest the *Fundamental Principles of 5S* video course. Use the coupon code "5SMadeEasy" during checkout to receive 10% off this video. You can find the video at: www.the5Sstore.com/5S-video-course.html.

Step 4: Play the 5S Nuts & Bolts Game developed by GBMP (Figure 4.1). This game's simple format will help drive home how 5S can remove stress and confusion with staff members while also improving product quality and customer satisfaction. Simulation games are a great way to learn concepts while also having some fun in a team setting. You can find this game at: www.the5Sstore.com/nuts-bolts-game.html and as with the video mentioned above, use the coupon code "5SMadeEasy" to save 10%.

Figure 4.1   5S Nuts & Bolts Game by GBMP (Newton, MA)

Tip

Be prepared to stop throughout the video to point out particular areas of inter-est and to field questions. As with the PowerPoint presentation, write any ideas into the "Team Ideas" section at the end of this chapter. Refer back to these ideas during the Set in Order step. Interactive viewing is key to making the group feel comfortable and enthusiastic about the endeavor.

Tips for Launch Success

Choose someone to take meeting minutes and notes during the entire event. Make sure to save these notes electronically for sharing during other rollouts. Utilize a 2′ × 3′ Post-it style pad and maybe an easel to keep track of the following:

■ 5S ideas that the team thought of during the PowerPoint and the video.
■ A running list of action items.
■ Team ideas.
■ Parking lot items (ideas or concerns that surface but are out of scope).
■ Materials list.
■ Lessons learned.
■ Take plenty of *before* pictures prior to beginning the event.
■ Capture a team picture.
■ Get everyone on the team to sign the Project Charter.

Note: There are also areas in each chapter to capture action items, parking lot ideas, and general notes.

Never forget that this is new for most if not all of the trainees. Be empathetic to their concerns and listen with sincerity. They are learning something new, and all learning curves start slowly.

Train the Team: Summary of Steps

☐ Use the *What, Why, Where, When,* and *How* format to explain what it is all about.
☐ Go through the PowerPoint presentation.
☐ Watch the 5S video.
☐ Play the 5S Nuts & Bolts Game.
☐ Conduct a Q&A session with the team.
☐ Capture team ideas.

Action Items

1. _____
2. _____
3. _____
4. _____
5. _____
6. _____

Team Ideas

1. _____
2. _____
3. _____
4. _____
5. _____
6. _____

Parking Lot Items

Ideas and issues out of scope but still worth capturing:

1. _____
2. _____
3. _____
4. _____
5. _____
6. _____

Chapter 5

Sort

By now if you have followed the steps in the other chapters you should have:

- A general idea as to what 5S is all about.
- An understanding of the benefits of 5S.
- A Project Charter.
- The team, project lead, scribe, and 5S champion in place.
- Determined the project schedule (i.e., a 4-day blitz or spread out over several weeks).
- Determined the workspace where 5S will be implemented.
- Communicated the general plan to all other departments (especially the facilities and maintenance departments).
- Trained the team on 5S concepts and reviewed the plan with them.
- A 2′ × 3′ Post-it style pad and easel for capturing action items and other notes.
- Plenty of *before* pictures.

If you have skipped any of the above items, I strongly suggest completing them in full prior to starting the Sort step.

Assuming those items are all done, let's move forward.

Imagine if you will, going through the utensil drawer in your home kitchen. Along with several spatulas, spoons, corn holders, corkscrews, and whisks, there is something sharp in there. But you are in that drawer digging, looking, searching for a bottle opener and, oops! You just sliced your finger on a knife. Stressful and unsafe—that is the type of situation that Sort helps eliminate for your employees.

Sort is the first of the five pillars of 5S. During this step you will go through the chosen area and remove everything not needed for current production. The more clutter you remove, the easier the next step, Set in Order, will be. Plus, it just simply makes the area easier and safer to work in. The tool most often used during the Sort process is a 5S red tag (see Figure 5.1a). The tag is used as a means to depict the status of an item that may or may not be needed in the area.

(a)

(b)

Figure 5.1 (a) Red Tag and (b) Red Tag Area Sign (Courtesy of The 5S Store, LLC, Pepperell, MA, and Accuform Signs, Brooksville, FL.)

The tagged items are then moved to a predetermined red tag area often labeled with a red tag area sign (see Figure 5.1b).

Estimated time to complete this step—1 to 3 hours, depending on the size of the area.

Benefits

- Removes clutter
- Saves money by finding missing tools, office supplies, and inventory
- Improves safety
- Improves space availability
- Improves workflow
- Improves productivity
- Reduces searching

Materials Needed

The materials needed are red tags, pens, red tag area sign, material handling carts, trash barrels, dumpster, safety glasses, and gloves.

Pre-Event Tasks

Develop a plan for what will be done with the material put in the red tag area. Some things to consider:

Who will have the final say on the disposition of items?

_____

How often will the red tag area be reviewed?

_____

Will you track red tagged items to help capture how much was saved or trashed?   ☐ Yes   ☐ No

Who will be held responsible for maintaining the 5S red tag area?

_____

Install a 5S Communication Board (for examples, see Figures 6.29 and 6.30 at the end of Chapter 6).

What will be done with the items that are no longer needed? Can any of the items be given to employees? Sold? Donated?

_____

_____

Red Tag Event Steps

Step 1: Write in the names of the people that attended the event:

_____   _____
_____   _____
_____   _____
_____   _____

Throughout the event remind the team that *all* unnecessary items are to be removed from the designated area. This means every single item must be considered. Go through the entire area, left to right, top to bottom.

Step 2: Review the benefits of the Sort process with the team. Determine the length of the event. Explain that the plan is to go through the entire area, opening all drawers, cabinets, shelves, and so on, and remove and tag everything that is not needed to do their daily tasks. Remind them that if they have duplicates of items, those should be removed too. For example, many people have several of the same screwdriver at their workstation when they really only need one. Remind the team to practice safety guidelines regarding bending, reaching, and lifting. It is also a good idea to wear safety glasses and gloves during the event.

Step 3: You will use preprinted blank red tags with fields to be filled in during the event. There are many areas on the form to be filled out. Make sure everyone has one form in their hands while you are discussing this step. Decide as a team what sections must be filled out. Take a tag and circle with a Sharpie those areas the team has decided are important. Keep that tag aside and handy for future reference.

Step 4: Begin the red tag event. Hand everyone a handful of red tags. Make sure you have an ample amount of red tags available. The last thing you want is to run out of tags. Be available to answer any questions that may arise.

Tip

After the initial event, place unused red tags in a 5S Red Tag Center (Figure 5.2) strategically placed throughout the facility (Figure 5.3).

For large facilities, place several of these red tag areas and 5S Red Tag Center signs throughout the plant to help reduce wasted travel time.

Figure 5.2 "5S Red Tag Center" Sign (Courtesy of The 5S Store, LLC, Pepperell, MA, and Accuform Signs, Brooksville, FL.)

Figure 5.3 Red Tag Area *after* a Sort Event (Courtesy of Macresco, Boston, MA.)

Step 5: Once the event is done, take *after* pictures from the same view as the *before* pictures as well as a picture of the now filled red tag area. Also, make sure to take a picture of the team in front of the area that the team just sorted through.

Step 6: Reconvene as a team in front of the red tag area. Discuss any thoughts and lessons learned for future red tag events. Capture action items and parking lot issues.

Estimated value of items removed: $_____
Estimated square footage saved by removing the unneeded items?
_____ sq. ft.

Lessons Learned for Future Red Tag Events

1. _____
2. _____
3. _____
4. _____
5. _____
6. _____
7. _____
8. _____
9. _____

Step 7: Using the "Before and After Template" (see: www.the5Sstore.com/ 5SMadeEasy) save your *before* and *after* pictures to the template and post the document on your 5S Communication Board.

Next Step—Set in Order and Shine. During this step you will arrange the tools and equipment at point of use, arrange visual controls, and set up daily 5-minute 5S routines.

Sort: Summary of Steps

☐ Write in the names of the people that attended the event.
☐ Review the benefits of Sort with the team.
☐ Quick review of how to fill out a 5S red tag properly.
☐ Start the red tag event.
☐ Take *after* photos of the area as well as the new red tag area.
☐ Discuss lessons learned with the team.
☐ Post your "before and after" document on your 5S Communication Board.

Action Items

Things that still need to be done:

1. _____
2. _____
3. _____
4. _____
5. _____
6. _____

Parking Lot Items

Ideas and issues out of scope but still worth capturing:

1. _____
2. _____
3. _____
4. _____
5. _____
6. _____

Notes

_____
_____
_____
_____
_____
_____
_____

Chapter 6

Set in Order and Shine

Summary

Have you ever lost your keys? You were ready to leave your house in a rush only to realize you cannot find your keys. Initially, you check all the normal areas and then concern sets in as the keys continue to elude you. You cannot find them. You get stressed; you start double and triple checking the same spot. If someone speaks to you, you are likely to respond somewhat harshly. Then, voila, the keys show up and all the stress and anxiety goes away. Life is good again except now you are late. Similar occurrences happen all day, every day on the manufacturing floor. The average worker spends 30% of his/her day searching, looking for tools and materials, or wondering what to do next. There is so much time wasted simply due to a lack of order. This is where *Set in Order,* the second pillar of 5S comes in, combined with the third pillar, *Shine.*

Set in Order is basically the process of arranging the work area so that tools, equipment, and materials are kept at the point of use, at the most appropriate distance with visual controls (labels and shadow boards) in place to make non-compliance (anything out of place) easily noticed. During these steps, you will go through the chosen area and arrange items such as tools, equipment, and supplies at the point of use and label them so *anyone* knows where the items belong. Moreover, you will clean up the area while putting processes in place to keep it looking clean and orderly.

Estimated time to complete this step—6 to 14 hours depending on the size and condition of the area.

Benefits

- Puts everything you need to do the job in plain sight just where you need it.
- Removes clutter.
- Reduces wasted time searching for items.
- Improves safety by removing tripping hazards.

■ Improves workspace availability.
■ Improves workflow.
■ Improves productivity.
■ Develops a standard of consistency for where and how items should be stored.
■ Develops a standard for how the area should look overall.
■ Reduces worker frustration from searching for lost or misplaced items.
■ Decreases defects by reducing the potential of using the wrong items or tools.
■ In a clean area it is easier to see maintenance problems such as oil leaks.
■ Provides a more appropriate and enjoyable work atmosphere.

Materials Needed

The materials needed are red tags, scissors, floor tape, pallet corners, trash barrel signs, tool shadow tape, pegboards and hooks, cable ties, Sharpies, label printer, magnetic 8 × 11 ticket holders, parts bins, sign maker, paint, paint brushes, cleaning supplies, brooms, dustpans, vacuum, rags, masking tape, material handling carts, trash barrels. (See the "5S Materials Checklist" at the end of this book.)

Take a Minute—Discuss some examples of where searching for an item has wasted time and hampered production.

Pre-Event Tasks

■ Take plenty of pictures of the area *before* you begin the event.
■ Have your 5S materials already in stock, organized, and laid out for ease of access. (See the "5S Materials Checklist" at the end of this book.) Some plants have a "5S Cart" with all of the 5S supplies on it.
■ Determine what colors will be used for certain material status. These colors are considered your 5S Color Visual Standards. (See an example of "5S Visual Standards" in Figure 6.1 and also in the "Forms" section at the end of

5S Visual Standards

Color Standard	Category	Description
Red	Hold/Quarantine	Rejects/Hold/Issues
Yellow	Warehouse Materials	Outgoing/Incoming Materials/Palletizing Areas
Green	Signals/Triggers	Kanban Locations
Blue	Tools & Accessories	Trash Cans, Pallet Jacks
Black/Yellow	Safety/Caution	Fire, PPE, Doorways
Black/White	Electrical	Electric Panels
Red/White	Warehouse Lanes	Walking Lanes/Travel Lanes

Figure 6.1 5S Visual Standards (Courtesy of The 5S Store, LLC, Pepperell, MA.)

this book. You can also download a template from the *5S Made Easy* page on The 5S Store website at: www.the5Sstore.com/5SMadeEasy.)

■ Speak to the facilities department and explain what you are doing. Review any heavy equipment or machinery that may need to be disconnected, moved, and de-energized for safety. Ask someone from facilities/maintenance to review lock-out/tag out safety procedures with your 5S team.

■ Determine if anything would require recalibration or re-leveling if it was moved and decide how that will be handled.

Tip

Keeping outside departments involved in your 5S implementation is a great way to improve buy-in for future expansion of the program.

Set in Order and Shine Steps

Step 1: Create a "Current State" spaghetti diagram (see Figure 6.2) of the workflow that goes through the area. This does not have to be pretty or to scale but should be a good representative of what goes on in the area in a typical day. Spaghetti diagrams help detail the actual physical movement of people and materials through a work process. This is simply a map showing all of the movement as the work is done step by step.

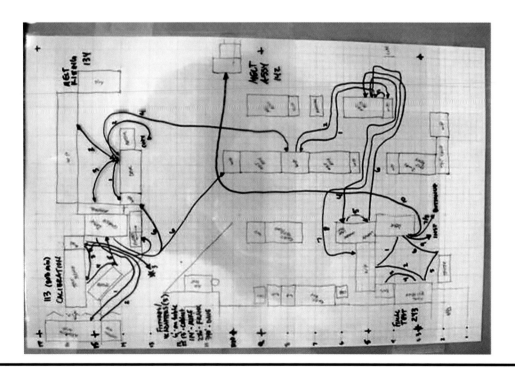

Figure 6.2   Current State Spaghetti Diagram (Courtesy of Macresco, Boston, MA.)

Step 2: Stand in a Circle Exercise. Our friends at Macresco, a Business Improvement Consultancy, utilize the Stand in a Circle Exercise originating from Taiichi Ohno. This is a great exercise for taking a focused approach at truly seeing what is occurring in the area. Ohno would draw a circle with a piece of chalk and then stand in the circle for hours. If training others, he would put them in the circle and then come back and ask what they learned through observation. The process is outlined below:

1. Find a safe spot to stand so you can easily see what is happening in the workplace. If possible, use a piece of chalk too and draw a circle to help prevent you from walking around.
2. Stand and observe the activity around you. It is very important to observe. In other words, do not comment or discuss what you are seeing at this point.
3. Write down at least 30 small problems or types of waste that you observe. Some examples are watching an operator strain to reach a tool or noticing a tripping hazard.
4. Review the findings with the team members.
5. Work with the team members to identify the type of waste or inefficiencies you have observed.
6. Identify the root cause of some of the items on the list by using the "Ask Why 5 Times" methodology. (See the box on the "5 Whys" process.)
7. Resolve at least one issue within the next 30 minutes. Prioritize safety or environmental issues.

Step 3: Discuss as a team some of the inefficiencies of the workflow. With no blinders on, discuss ideas on how the flow could be improved. Your goal is to make the workflow easy, and easy to see if it is flowing or backed up.

Try to straighten out the twisted spaghetti path of your current state. The ideal flow is work flowing in a counter-clockwise "U" shape similar to what you see in Figure 6.3.

The idea is that if you stood in the center of this upside-down "U" shape, you could see all workstations. You could easily see where the workflow was backed up. Then you could respond quickly to help solve the problem. This is part of visual management of the workplace.

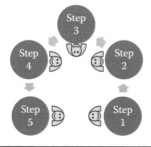

Figure 6.3 The Ideal Process Flow (Courtesy of The 5S Store, LLC, Pepperell, MA.)

The other idea is that if workers were standing at workstations on the inside of this upside-down "U," they would be using their dominant right hand to begin the work that flows to them from their right side. Again, this is the 5S idea of making the work easier.

Here is another example of a "before and after" spaghetti diagram to improve flow in a shipping and receiving area in a tight, low ceiling, industrial building (see Figure 6.4a,b).

Notice the difference in the two images. We actually removed some walls. All too often people do not think about the fact that walls can

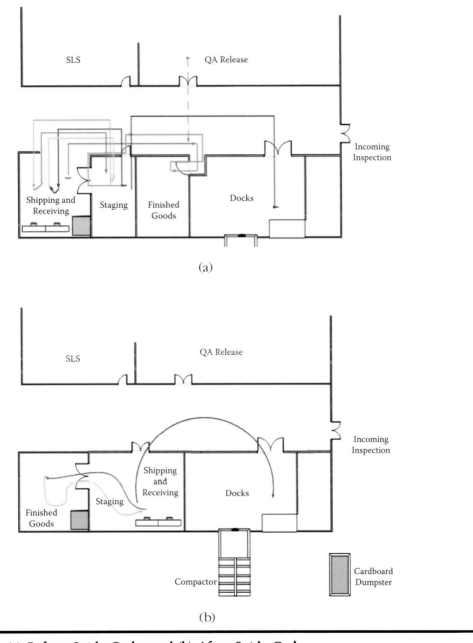

Figure 6.4   (a) *Before***: Set in Order and (b)** *After***: Set in Order**

5 WHYS

The most basic form of root cause analysis involves asking *why* five times to get to the root of a problem.* For example:

1. *Why* was the order late? Because it was missing a part.
2. *Why* was the part missing? Because the machine was broken.
3. *Why* was the machine broken? Because the brushes on the motor were bad.
4. *Why* were the brushes bad? Because they had not been replaced.
5. *Why* had they not been replaced? Because they are not on our preventative maintenance schedule.

---

* Courtesy of Bruce Hamilton and Pat Wardwells from GBMP (Newton, MA) and their book *e2 Continuous Improvement System*.

usually be removed. They were there for some other reason that no longer makes sense. This company just kept using existing space as they grew without making it fit their true needs thus imposing significant flow constraints. Once the walls came down the material and people flowed much more smoothly.

Brainstorm ideas for removing barriers to flow. Money is not an issue, time is not an issue. Simply get all the ideas written down and discussed. Also consider ways to improve ergonomics and reduce twisting, turning, bending, and reaching as much as possible.

Team Ideas

1. _____
2. _____
3. _____
4. _____
5. _____
6. _____
7. _____
8. _____
9. _____

Some Idea Examples

- Relocating or removing benches, cabinets, and shelves
- Utilizing more vertical space
- Tearing up old floors
- Removing walls

- Adding windows
- Adding power outlets
- Replacing old, worn-out equipment
- Adding retractable air hoses

Relocate workstations in the sequence of the workflow. (Recommended: U-shape arrangement with a counter-clockwise workflow. Standing in the middle, you can easily see whether the work is flowing smoothly or getting backed up at one of the workstations.)

Tip

Make sure to capture these ideas on paper and save the information in your binder.

Step 3a: Once you have designed a new layout of the work area, determine how and where to locate your tools, supplies, dies, documents, work in progress (WIP), inventory and anything else that needs to be in the area. Once you have decided the how and where, you will use visual controls to communicate the new standards. Some examples:

- Mount durable pegboard so you can hang tools and get them off of bench tops.
- For tools that are vertically mounted, utilize tool shadow tape.
- For tools that will be stored in drawers, use tool foam shadow boards.
- Use floor tape or floor corners to mark where the trash cans should go. Make sure to put a label on the floor as well, that says "Trash" or "Trash Can."
- For documents that must be visible, hang them in a magnetic, adhesive, or plain 8 × 11 job ticket holder.
- In Figure 6.5, we not only completely refinished the tabletop but also put tools at point of use.
- Store items in the sequence that they are used.
- Use retractable cords for suspending tools from the ceiling.
- Replace bolts requiring a wrench with hand-turned grip bolts, thus eliminating the wrench.
- Color coordinate tools with where they are used on the equipment.

Tip

When labeling items and producing signs or notices, set a standard and make sure that the same font, color, and type of holder is used everywhere.

Tip

As we discussed in Chapter 4: "Train the Team," it is important that the people that are working in the area be the ones to Set in Order and Shine their area.

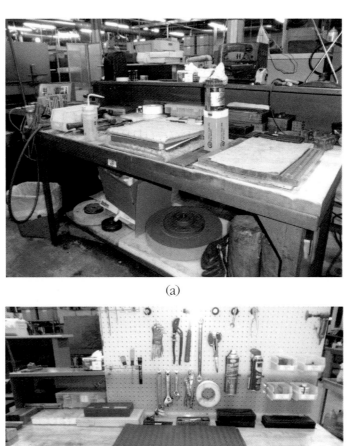

(a)

(b)

Figure 6.5 (a) *Before*: Set in Order and (b) *After*: The Tabletop Was Not Only Refinished But the Tools Were Also Put at Point of Use (Courtesy of Macresco, Boston, MA.)

Tip

You can find hundreds of Set in Order pictures and ideas at: www.5SBestPractices. com.

As a leader you must protect yourself from yourself. Be extremely careful not to force the layout or your ideas on the workers. Support them, empower them, let them figure it out. "Doing it to them" misses the point of 5S by a long shot. Figures 6.6 through 6.18 are some Set in Order, Shine, and point of use examples and ideas along with several "before and after" pictures.

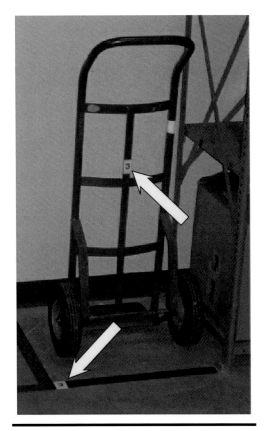 

Figure 6.6 Set in Order: Numbered 3 Wheeler Matched to Numbered Space for It (Courtesy of The 5S Store, LLC, Pepperell, MA.)

Figure 6.7 Aisle Marking for Clear Travel Lanes and Improved Safety (Courtesy of The 5S Store, LLC, Pepperell, MA.)

Figure 6.8 Aisle Marking for Clear Travel Lanes and Improved Safety (Courtesy of Aerodyne Alloys, South Windsor, CT.)

(a)

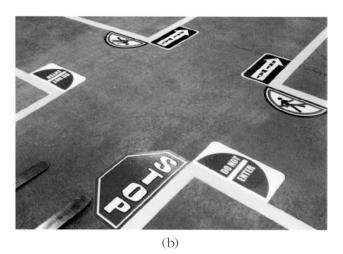

(b)

Figure 6.9 (a) Floor Signs and (b) Aisle Marking for Clear Travel Lanes and Improved Safety (Courtesy of The 5S Store, LLC, Pepperell, MA, and Accuform Signs, Brooksville, FL.)

Figure 6.10   Cardboard Kanban

Figure 6.11   Tape Kanban (Courtesy of Macresco, Boston, MA.)

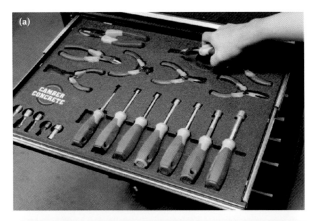

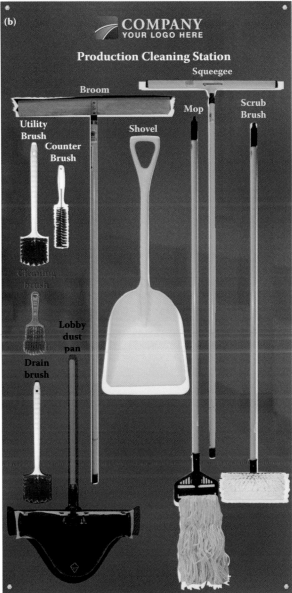

Figure 6.12 (a) Visual Tool Drawers: Tool Shapes in the Foam Show Where Each Tool Belongs; (b) Visual Boards for Cleaning Tools; (c) Visual Boards for Personal Protective Equipment (Courtesy of The 5S Store, LLC, Pepperell, MA, and Accuform Signs, Brooksville, FL.)

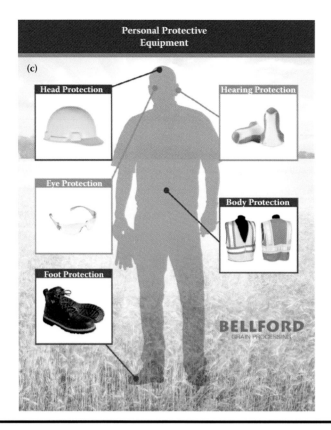

Figure 6.12 (Continued) (a) Visual Tool Drawers: Tool Shapes in the Foam Show Where Each Tool Belongs; (b) Visual Boards for Cleaning Tools; and (c) Visual Boards for Personal Protective Equipment (Courtesy of The 5S Store, LLC, Pepperell, MA, and Accuform Signs, Brooksville, FL.)

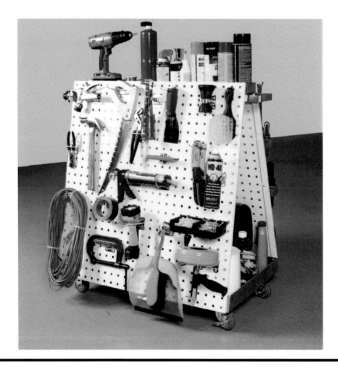

Figure 6.13 Organized Mobile Tool Control (Courtesy of The 5S Store, LLC, Pepperell, MA, and Triton Products, Solon, OH.)

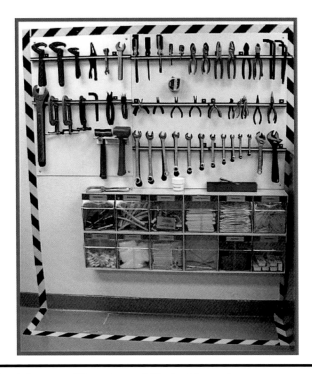

Figure 6.14 Wall Tool Storage (Courtesy of Kevin Meyer.)

Figure 6.15 Visual Recycle Area: Color Coding for Where Each Bin Belongs (Courtesy of Fuss & O'Neill, Boston, MA.)

Figure 6.16   Floor Marking for Setting Standards (Courtesy of The 5S Store, LLC, Pepperell, MA, and Ergomat, Lorain, OH.)

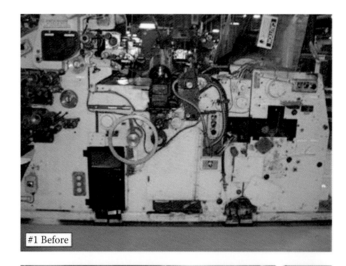

Figure 6.17   *Before* and *After* Shine Event (Courtesy of Western States Envelope & Label, Milwaukee, WI.)

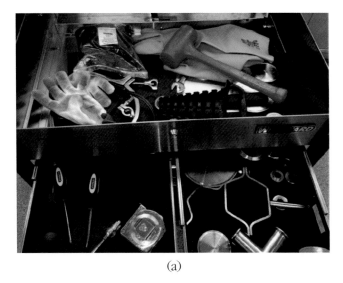

(a)

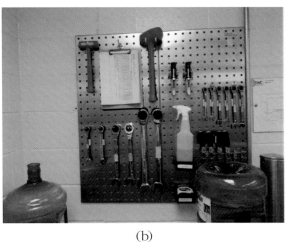

(b)

Figure 6.18 (a) *Before* and (b) *After* (Courtesy of Southwest Cheese, Clovis, NM.)

LESSONS FROM THE FIELD

One company we worked with had a 100-year-old plant and all the grunge buildup as well. Initially, when we began the Set in Order and Shine phases, we just figured we would reorganize, clean the equipment a little, and improve the overall appearance of the area. As the team began working, someone suggested we paint the walls. The walls that were supposed to be white were now gray and filthy. What a great idea. Next, someone suggested tearing up the old floor and laying down an epoxy. Wow. At first I thought this was a little extreme but the more I thought about it, the more I liked the enthusiasm. Some of the improvements from our first day are shown in Figures 6.20 and 6.21. The point of this story is that no idea for improvement should be cast aside. All options should be open for discussion and considered.

Step 3b: During this step, you will also focus on Shine whereby all equipment will look as good as new when you are done. You need to scrub all equipment, walls, floors, doors, windowsills, cabinets—everything.

Some Shine Idea Examples

- Paint equipment
- Paint walls
- Clean windows
- Scrub or replace old keyboards
- Replace or refinish workshop benches
- Clean all tools

Tip

Have Opportunity, Maintenance, and Repair Request tags available. When your team sees oil leaks, broken parts, or frayed wiring, they can write up a Repair Request on the spot (Figure 6.19).

Figure 6.19 Opportunity Tag (Courtesy of The 5S Store, LLC, Pepperell, MA, and used with permission of TheVisualMachine.com, Columbus, NC, 2015.)

Floor Before   Floor After

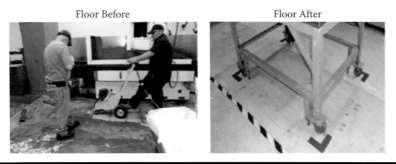

Figure 6.20 Floor: *Before* and *After*

Walls Before   Walls After

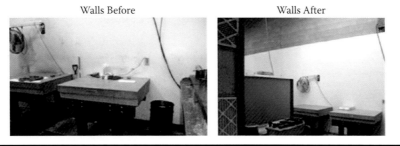

Figure 6.21 Walls: *Before* and *After* (Courtesy of Macresco, Boston, MA.)

Before   After

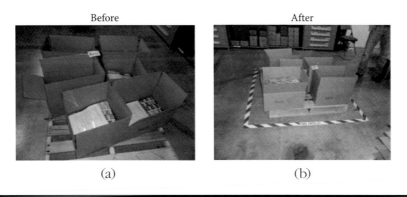

(a)   (b)

Figure 6.22 (a) *Before* and (b) *After* (Courtesy of Inland Packaging, Lauderhill, FL.)

Tip

If you foresee a lot of maintenance work, ask that someone from the plant maintenance department be a part of your 5S team.

Step 4: Develop visual controls for equipment wherever possible to make abnormal situations visible at a glance (see Figure 6.22a,b).

Some Idea Examples

■ Gauge marking labels   ■ Temperature indicator strips
■ Torque seal   ■ Zebra cards

Some examples of "before and after" 5S are shown in Figures 6.17 through 6.28.

(a)

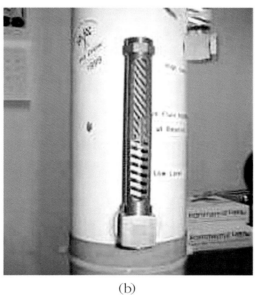

(b)

Figure 6.23   (a) Gauge Marking Label and (b) Zebra Card (Courtesy of The 5S Store, LLC, Pepperell, MA, and used with permission of TheVisualMachine.com, Columbus, OH, 2015.)

Step 5: Collect whatever 5S materials are remaining and store them in a designated location. Set up kanbans for all of these materials as well as anything you ran out of but may need again.

Step 6: Once the event is done, take *after* pictures from the same view as the *before* pictures.

Step 7: Create a "5S Before and After" template and upload the files to your folder on your company's server as discussed in Chapter 3: "Develop Your Plan." Print this out and put it in your binder in the Set in Order/Shine section and post the improvement images on your 5S Communication Board (see a few 5S board examples in Figures 6.29 and 6.30).

Before

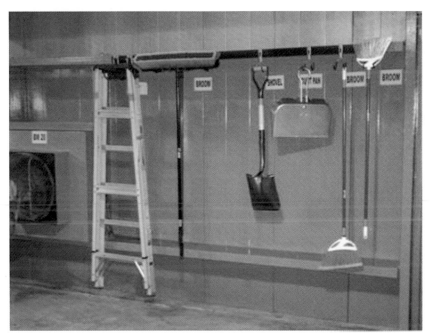

After

Figure 6.24 Example 1—Set in Order: *Before* **and** *After* **(Courtesy of Hexion, www.hexion. com.)**

Step 8: Reconvene as a team in front of the new clean and organized area. Discuss any thoughts, concerns, or ideas. Capture action items and parking lot issues.

Next Step—Standardize. Make everything you have done into a habit to help ensure the operation does not go back to the way it used to be.

Before

After

Figure 6.25 Example 2—Set in Order: *Before* **and** *After* **(Courtesy of Hexion, www.hexion. com.)**

Before

After

Figure 6.26   Example 1—Set in Order and Shine: *Before* and *After* **(Courtesy of Southwest Cheese, Clovis, NM.)**

Before

After

Figure 6.27 Example 2—Set in Order and Shine: *Before* **and** *After* **(Courtesy of TREMCO, Beachwood, OH.)**

Before

After

Figure 6.28   Example 3—Set in Order and Shine: *Before* **and** *After* **(Courtesy of Collins Bus Corporation, South Hutchinson, KS.)**

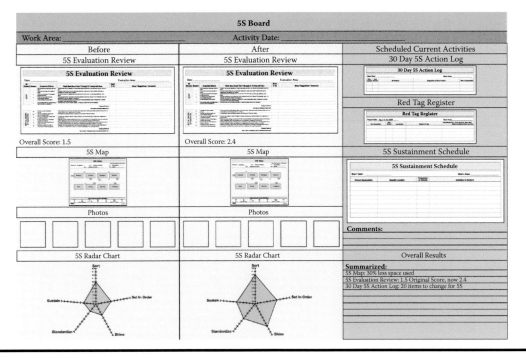

Figure 6.29   Example 1: 5S Communication Board (Courtesy of The 5S Store, LLC, Pepperell, MA, and Enna Products, Bellingham, WA.)

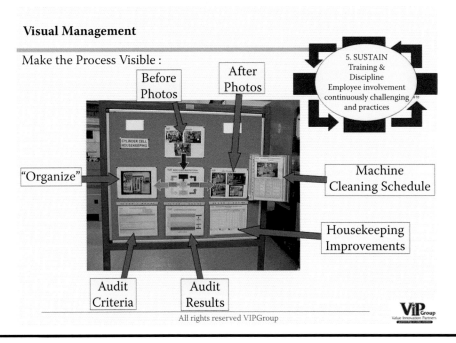

Figure 6.30   Example 2: 5S Communication Board (Courtesy of the VIP Group, Lake St. Louis, MO.)

Set in Order: Summary of Steps

- ☐ Create your current state spaghetti diagram.
- ☐ Stand in a Circle Exercise.
- ☐ Discuss flow challenges with the team.
- ☐ Determine how and where to lay out your tools and equipment and get this step done.
- ☐ Conduct Shine while setting everything in order.
- ☐ Store unused 5S materials in the designated cabinet, shelf, room, and so on.
- ☐ Take *after* pictures and post them.
- ☐ Team discussion.

> **Tip**
>
> Implement a kanban card system for the 5S supplies. One of the quickest ways to kill momentum of a 5S initiative is to run out of 5S supplies. If you need help with this, just contact The 5S Store at: (978)-842-4610 or e-mail: CustomerService@the5Sstore.com.

Action Items

1. _____
2. _____
3. _____
4. _____
5. _____
6. _____

Team Ideas

1. _____
2. _____
3. _____
4. _____
5. _____
6. _____
7. _____
8. _____

Parking Lot Items

Ideas and issues out of scope but still worth capturing:

1. _____
2. _____
3. _____
4. _____

Chapter 7

Standardize

Standardize is the fourth pillar of 5S. During this step you will set up processes that help make non-compliance obvious.

This is a significant step that should not be taken lightly. Without sufficient standards, people will not know what is expected of them. Setting clear expectations is the only way to have a successful 5S program.

This may seem like an obvious standard to put into place; however, I have seen this one simple standard missed countless times. Make it easy on everyone and remove ambiguity by posting your color standards throughout the facility.

Note: I have been asked often if there is a set color standard for 5S. The answer is no. Many companies follow OSHA (Occupational Safety & Health Administration standards) for their safety requirements; however, this misses the mark for kanban, equipment, trash, and so on. See our suggested color standards in Chapter 6 "Set in Order and Shine" or in the "Forms" section at the end of this book.

Estimated time to complete this step—3 hours.

LESSONS FROM THE FIELD

One company I worked with (a defense contractor you would surely know) had color standards; however, it was assumed that everyone knew what they were. During the initial tour, I asked, "Do you have color standards and if so are they posted? It appears there is some consistency throughout the plant, however, I've occasionally seen different colors used for floor pallet markers." The customer responded, "Yes, we do have color standards. They're not posted, however, every new employee is trained on the standards when they go through orientation." I suggested that they post these standards in various locations throughout the facility, as there is a lot to remember during the first day of orientation the least of which is what color to use for the work in progress (WIP).

Benefits

- Problems of the past will not resurface.
- Develops consistency for where and how items should be stored.
- Provides a foundation for clear expectations.
- Reduces uncertainty about how the area should look.
- Provides a foundation so all documents, signs, and labeling are consistent in appearance.
- Allows the workers to know what is expected (absolutely *key* for 5S success).
- Makes abnormal conditions obvious at a glance.

Take a Minute—Discuss some examples of where the lack of a standard caused a problem for you in the past and ideas on how to correct it from reoccurring.

Materials Needed

The materials needed are a 5S Area Audit form, 5S Shine Map, 5S Maintenance Chart, How to Develop a Successful 5S Audit Program, Weekly 5S Audit Score sheet, and Opportunity tags.

Pre-Event Tasks

Make enough copies of the 5S Audit form and 5S Maintenance Chart for the entire team being trained.

Standardize Steps

Step 1: Develop your 5S Shine Map. To do this, draw a quick and easy map of the area showing major lanes and equipment for reference points.

Step 2: Break your 5S Shine Map into quadrants and assign each team member that works in that area a quadrant to keep clean and orderly and to inspect the equipment daily. The key here is to make sure to hold each member accountable for their area. We will discuss how to do this shortly.

Step 3: Discuss and develop a 5S Maintenance Chart[*] (see Figure 7.1). This chart helps to standardize and sustain the previous 5S pillars along with improving equipment productivity.

---

[*] Courtesy of Macresco, Boston, MA.

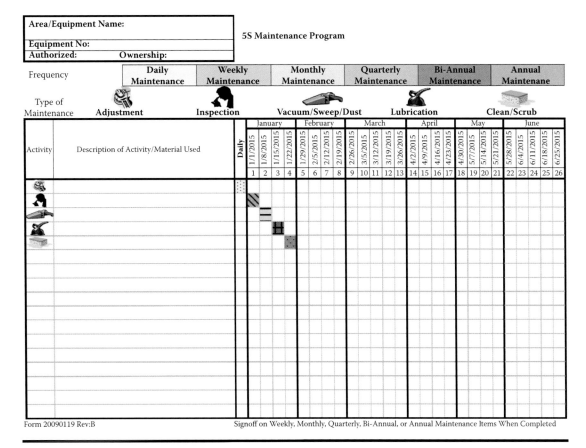

Figure 7.1 5S Maintenance Chart (Courtesy of Macresco, Boston, MA.)

Benefits

- Clarifies expectations
- Empowers employees
- Provides a method for organizing necessary activities
- Provides feedback at a glance
- Helps to ensure the proper maintenance is conducted on machinery and workspaces
- Fill in the following for each quadrant:
  - Name of team member responsible for that quadrant
    List the areas to be cleaned
  - List equipment maintenance tasks
- Categorize all activities into one of five categories:
  - Adjustment
  - Inspection
  - Vacuum/Sweep/Dust
  - Lubrication
  - Clean/Scrub
- Determine how often each activity needs to occur

Tip

Consider ways to eliminate the need for cleaning in the first place. For example, if wood shavings are getting on the floor, install a vacuum nearby that automatically collects the shavings as they are produced.

Step 4: Discuss the 5S Audit Program and its benefits.

Defined: A 5S Audit Program is a tool used for measuring the improvements that have been made. Well-managed audits help drive root cause analysis and long lasting corrective actions. 5S Audits are one of the most useful tools to set expectations, standards, and a means to hold people accountable. The audit scores also can provide routine feedback to your team—a key part of sustaining your improvements (more on this in Chapter 8: "Sustain").

A word of caution, however—audits are often improperly used. If audits are used only to *punish* people for non-conformance, then several undesirable (but predictable) side effects will occur:

People will learn to "pencil whip" the audit. That is, they will check off everything as completed without actually walking around and looking to see if it is completed. It becomes a form to fill out and file instead of a tool for sustaining and improving.

People will learn to do "just enough to get by." That is, they will do just enough to get just enough points or percentage on the audit score that they will not be punished. They will not give their full effort and will not be motivated to look for more ways to improve.

To avoid these bad side effects, use audit scores for *feedback, recognition,* and *goal setting:* "We averaged 75% (out of the total possible point totals) this week on our 5S Audit [*feedback*]. That is an improvement over last week's average of 70%. Good [*recognition*]. Let's set a goal to average 80% next week [*goal setting*]."

Benefits of 5S Audits

- Clarifies expectations.
- Empowers employees.
- Provides feedback on the areas and processes that *do* meet or exceed standards.
- Provides feedback on the areas that have fallen *below* expectations.
- Provides a forum to capture root cause and corrective actions that will help your team make continuous improvement a part of their daily work.

Step 5: Review the 5S Audit form with the team (see Figure 7.2). Make sure everyone has a copy of the 5S Audit form.

5S Audit Checklist

Status	Rating Level	# of Non-Conformities
Poor	1	5 or More
Fair	2	3–4
Good	3	2
Very Good	4	1
Best Practice	5	None

Audit Date:
Auditor(S):

Area:

Category		Score	Comments/Observations
Sort	**Objective: Determine What Is and Isn't Needed**		
	No unneeded equipment, tools, paperwork, etc., are present in area		
	All necessary items are clearly labeled		
	No unneeded inventory, supplies, parts, or materials (WIP) present in area		
	Personal items are not cluttering work area: tripping dangers are removed		
	Red Tag system is in place and unnecessary items are tagged and stored	0	
Set in Order	**Objective: A Place for Everything and Everything in Its Place**		
	Designated areas are visually identified for finished, WIP, and pending jobs		
	Tools are at point of use and storage is visual (easy to see, retrieve, return)		
	Aisles, work areas, benches, equipment are clearly and consistently marked		
	Storage is above knees and below shoulders: work is at correct height		
	Paperwork and documents are properly organized and labeled	0	
Shine	**Objective: Clean to Inspection**		
	Floors, walls, stairs, surfaces, equipment are free of dirt, oil, grime and clutter		
	A maintenance system is in place to ensure periodic equipment inspection		
	Cleaning materials are well organized and easily accessible		
	Area is well lit and ventilated, labels and signs are legible/in good condition:		
	Shine responsibilities are clear and monitored regularly	0	
Standardize	**Objective: Standards to Keep the First 3 S's from Deteriorating**		
	5S Maintenance Schedule and Checklist are posted in the area		
	5S Visual Color Standards are posted and followed		
	Standard Work Instructions are posted		
	5S and continuous improvement results are posted and clear		
	Processes exist to monitor previous Audit Action items	0	
Sustain	**Objective: Make It a Habit**		
	5S Audits are conducted regularly		
	Supervisors are actively involved in 5S activities		
	Management conducts regularly scheduled gemba walks		
	All employees are trained in 5S and engaged to maintain the 5S Standard		
	Communication Boards are up to date	0	
	Total Score (of the above 25 boxes)	0	

Figure 7.2 5S Audit Checklist (Courtesy of GBMP, Newton, MA.)

Step 6: Conduct your first audit as a team. Have everyone walk along the same path and write down their scores for each section. Then, discuss everyone's score and how they determined them. This is a critical step for making the audit objective and fact based (versus subjective and opinion based). There is always some unavoidable subjectivity between a score of a 2 or 3, 3 or 4, and so on. This is a critical step for beginning to set standards. Talk as a group and determine the various scoring results.

One easy way to standardize this process is to create a scoring matrix that is based on the number of non-compliances (see Figure 7.2, a sample "5S Audit Checklist"). If any two people on the team disagree on the number of non-conformities, stop and talk about it. See the potential scenario that follows, which helps explain the need to talk among the group:

Team Leader: Fred, you called this grease fitting a non-conformity, but Mary did not. Why?
Fred: It has excess grease smeared all over the machine cover. When I close the cover after my inspection, grease gets on my hand and then gets on the units I'm assembling. Grease on the units means they'll be rejected by Quality Assurance. Then they'll be sent back to be cleaned up. That's rework.
Team Leader: Mary, what do you say?
Mary: I did not know the grease would cause rework. I now agree with Fred. Excess grease at the grease fitting is a non-conformity.

With the team now in agreement about how to score the grease fitting, your audit scores will all turn out the same. Moreover, making notes of these non-conformities will help drive corrective actions.

A sample of this Audit form is shown in Figure 7.2 and can be downloaded on the *5S Made Easy* page on The 5S Store website. This first audit should take at least an hour to allow for discussion about making sure everyone scores the same way. Take your time. Going forward, audits will likely take under 30 minutes.

Step 7: Once your audit is complete, agree as a team what the final score is for each section and update the Audit form. This score will be your baseline for future audits. Your score will likely be low, as you are just beginning. Every time the score improves, give the team some positive recognition. Let them know you have noticed their work has paid off with higher 5S Audit Scores.

Step 8: Add that score to the Weekly 5S Audit Score Graph which should roll up to the Monthly Dept. 5S Scorecard (see Figure 7.3). Post the graph on the team's 5S Communication Board in the area. A graph allows you to see progress and trends. The team will take satisfaction in seeing improving

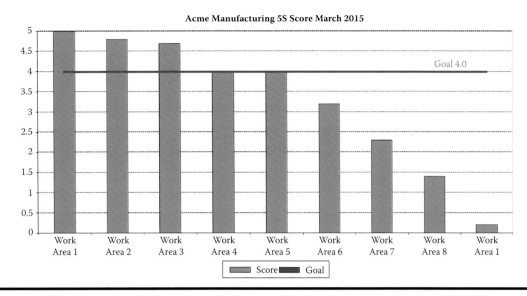

Figure 7.3 Monthly Dept. 5S Scorecard

scores. Declining scores will result in team members asking, "What are we missing?" or "How can we improve?" This becomes a self-correcting process. It eliminates the need for anyone to chastise or point out what they've done wrong.

They can see it for themselves on the graph, and can get details from the 5S Audit Checklist. This data should also roll up to a Plant-Wide Monthly 5S Scorecard (see Figure 7.4). Some companies also chart the scores per 5S pillar (Sort, Set in Order, Shine, Standardize, Sustain). You will have to determine for yourself whether that is necessary. On the one hand, it may help to see which of these five areas needs the most improvement. Personally, I think this is overanalyzing the data and therefore provides no real value.

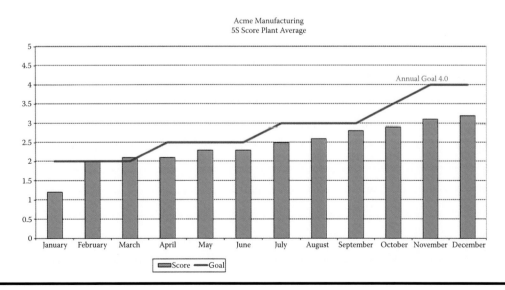

Figure 7.4 Plant-Wide Monthly 5S Scorecard

Note: Another key aspect that needs to be standardized is your 5S training process. This book has been created to give you an easy-to-duplicate 5S implementation plan and therefore standardize your training. You may choose to do things a little differently than the book suggests. This is absolutely fine: just make sure to make those changes the new standard.

Next Step—Sustain. Building the daily routines needed to follow through on all the improvements. Sustaining makes following the standard procedures a habit.

Standardize: Summary of Steps

- ☐ Develop your 5S Shine Map.
- ☐ Break your 5S Shine Map into quadrants and assign each team member.
- ☐ Discuss and develop a 5S Maintenance Chart.
- ☐ Discuss the 5S Audit program including the benefits along with a review of the Audit form and scoring.
- ☐ Conduct a 5S Audit.
- ☐ Review the results of the audit with the team and discuss scoring.
- ☐ Enter the scores into the 5S Audit Score Graph.
- ☐ Post the graph on the 5S Success whiteboard.

Action Items

1. _____
2. _____
3. _____
4. _____
5. _____
6. _____

Parking Lot Items

Ideas and issues out of scope but still worth capturing:

1. _____
2. _____
3. _____
4. _____
5. _____
6. _____

Chapter 8

Sustain

Summary

Sustain is the fifth and final pillar of 5S. It incorporates the disciplines needed to maintain the improvements. Sustaining makes the process of maintaining standardized procedures engrained in the normal operation of the business. Be forewarned that it is considered to be the most difficult of the 5S pillars.

Most companies succeed with the first three of the 5S pillars: Sort, Set in Order, and Shine and some companies do okay with Standardizing their processes. However, many have trouble sustaining the improvements. Ironically, it is actually a lot easier than most think. However, what is easy is not always put into practice. Moreover, as self-improvement guru Jim Rohn says, "What's easy to do, is also easy NOT to do."

Many companies struggle with Sustaining due to a lack of a true "why." They must decide why they want 5S to succeed in the first place. Many use 5S to organize and clean the area. This reason misses the intent by a long shot. While a successful 5S System certainly results in a cleaner, more organized workspace, it more importantly helps to solidify a culture of improvement and empowerment. What do I mean by *empowerment?* Instead of saying, "somebody ought to...," your team says, "let's try this..." 5S puts the power of improvement in the hands of the workers. It allows them to try, fail, react, and improve, which are the steps of learning. 5S develops their capacity to experiment with improvements systematically. Regrettably, many senior-level managers do not understand how valuable this benefit truly is. If they did, they would make 5S a priority. The 5S process allows people to teach themselves how to improve the workflow.

With that said, this chapter will focus on methods to systematically Sustain the improvements your team has made with their 5S program.[*]

---

[*] My thanks to my colleague Michael McCarthy, author of *Sustain Your Gains*, for his contributions to this chapter.

Benefits

1. Improvements will last and deliver the gains—the cost reductions and quicker production times that give you a competitive advantage.
2. Equipment will remain running efficiently (greater percentage of uptime).
3. The workforce will realize that the management team is serious about continuous improvement and follow their lead.
4. Morale will improve, because people prefer to work in an organized and clean workspace.
5. Safety improvements will remain intact.
6. Employees will feel empowered and realize they have some control over their work environment.
7. Now that tools and supplies are not misplaced, there will be a reduction of replacement spending.

Take a Minute—Discuss some ideas on how to sustain the team's improvements.

Materials Needed

The materials needed are a 5S Newsletter, 5S Management Walk Cards, 5S Message Board, 5S pens, 5S posters, 5S team shirts, and 5S banners.

Pre-Event Tasks

Schedule a monthly 5S program review with 5S team leaders. As the leader, you need to create the right conditions to help sustain your improvements. Developing these conditions is covered in detail within each Sustain step below. The necessary conditions are:

- *Knowledge*—Help everyone learn what 5S is all about and its benefits.
- *Time*—People need to have the time to do 5S activities.
- *Plan*—There needs to be a plan on how, when, and who will do activities.
- *Support*—Provide training, leadership, and recognition. Whether it is a formal recognition program or not, recognition to team members for their 5S efforts, delivered by you (the area supervisor or 5S champion) is part of the methodology of Sustain. It is a link in the Sustain chain that you cannot break without the whole Sustain process breaking.
- *Fun and enthusiasm*—Where possible make it fun and enthusiasm will follow.

Keep these ideas in mind while developing the Sustain steps below.

Sustain Steps

Step 1: Now that the 5S reorganization is complete, one useful idea is to get everyone to sign a 5S banner (see Figure 8.1) as a commitment to maintaining the 5S Audit standards that everyone has agreed to. You can find these at: www.the5Sstore.com/5SMadeEasy. At checkout, use the coupon code "5SMadeEasy" and get 10% off your purchase.

Step 2: Incorporate some visual management reminders for your team to do the 5S activities daily. See Figure 8.2 for some examples.

Step 3: Develop methods of communicating the status of the 5S program.
- *Some ideas:*
  - Install 5S Audit Results throughout the plant.
  - Hand out 5S message pens (Figure 8.3).
  - Include 5S updates in quarterly meetings and top executive meetings.
  - Create a weekly 5S newsletter (see: www.the5Sstore.com/5SMadeEasy for a template).
  - Ensure each 5S champion holds weekly 5S briefings with their department (see the "5S Team Weekly Meeting" form in the "Forms" section at the end of this book).
- *Some ideas for additional feedback:* Adhesive management walk cards (green cards to post at the location where 5S standards were followed, orange cards to post where improvement is needed) (Figure 8.4):

Step 4: Develop and maintain 5S status boards showing the 5S team members along with "before and after" pictures and activities (Figure 8.5).

Step 5: Develop a recognition program in order to make it fun and help Sustain. Much has been written and discussed as to whether it is necessary to have a recognition program that rewards 5S efforts. Here are some guidelines from my colleague Michael McCarthy, an expert in the use of rewards and recognition and the author of *Sustain Your Gains—The People Side of Lean–Six Sigma*, available at www.the5Sstore.com (see Figure 8.6).

Using these guidelines, you can decide how much recognition you need to plan, if any. Another tip from McCarthy: Avoid tangible rewards (cash, gifts, time off). Tangible rewards generally create competition among teammates, a work pattern of doing "just enough" to get the reward, and resentment from those who do not earn the rewards.

Figure 8.1 5S Team Commitment Banner (Courtesy of The 5S Store, LLC, Pepperell, MA, and Accuform Signs, Brooksville, FL.)

(a)

(b)

Figure 8.2 **(a) 5S Poster and (b) 5S T-Shirt (Courtesy of Lean Posters, www.leanposters.com, and The 5S Store, LLC, Pepperell, MA.)**

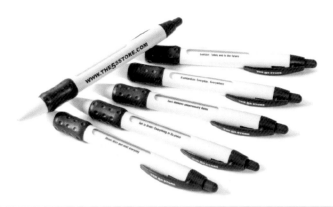

Figure 8.3   5S Message Pens

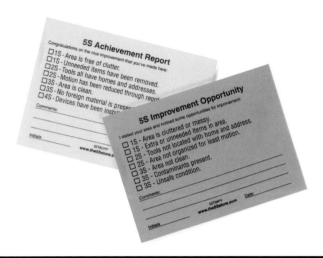

Figure 8.4   Management Walk Cards (Courtesy of The 5S Store, LLC, Pepperell, MA and GBMP, Newton, MA.)

If you want to reward and celebrate achievement of Sustain goals on 5S standards, McCarthy recommends:

Symbolic rewards that have "trophy" value (a.k.a. "bragging rights"). Examples are *wearables*: hats, patches, t-shirts, pins, and so on, that show the achievement. The hat or patch might read: "5S Sustainer: 13 Weeks." When upper management sees these hats or patches, they know who to give recognition to, and for what achievement (see Figure 8.7).

Caution

Do not simply *give out* these items. They must be *earned* by achieving the stated goal. For example, "When we sustain our 5S standards at 95% for 6 out of 8 weeks, everyone on the team will earn a '5S Sustainers' pin." When earned, these items have value and will be respected. If given out *un*-earned, these items will be considered *freebies* that do not mean anything and lose their value.

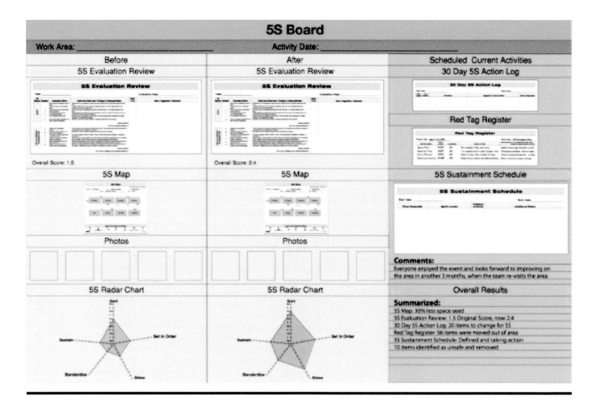

Figure 8.5   5S Board (Courtesy of The 5S Store, LLC, Pepperell, MA, and Enna Products, Bellingham, WA.)

You need more recognition when:	You need less recognition when:
There are fewer visual cues for the new standard work	Visual cues lead you through every step of the new standard work
There are no posted checklists to follow	Checklists to follow are posted
The new assembly sequence is not obvious	The shape of the parts make the new assembly sequence obvious
The new work sequence is significantly different than the old	The new work sequence is not that much different than the old one
Certain steps are frequently missed or done incorrectly	Most steps are done consistently
A new person or outsider cannot perform the new work steps without being told or guided	A new person or outsider can perform nearly all new work steps without being told or guided

Figure 8.6   Reward and Recognition Guidelines (Courtesy of Michael McCarthy.)

Figure 8.7   Reward Pins (Courtesy of The 5S Store, LLC, Pepperell, MA.)

Celebrations for sustaining a high percentage of 5S standards over a number of weeks or months. Your celebration might include a meal or refreshments (coffee and doughnuts, a cake or cookies or soft drinks). At the celebration, be sure to say *what* you are celebrating. "We did it! We sustained our 5S standards at 95% for 10 out of 13 weeks!"

At celebrations, ask team members "How did we do this?" or "Joe, tell us your secret for how you sustained a high 5S score on 5S Audits?" In this way, team members re-live their accomplishment, while simultaneously re-teaching themselves what it takes to sustain a high percentage on 5S standards.

Ask team members to come with you during your audits. Usually there is a "set up time" at the beginning of the shift when work materials are prepared. That is when one team member can begin to help you do the 5S audit. After 3 to 4 weeks, you can begin to let these team members do the audit without you and post the score on the graph. You can also begin to ask them to do the briefing about the graph at the shift meeting once a week. In this way, you gradually transfer ownership of the process to the team members themselves. The desired outcome is that the sustaining Audits, Recognition, and Feedback become a self-sustaining part of the team's daily routine, operating without you. They audit themselves, give themselves the feedback, and give themselves the recognition. This is the ideal state for Sustain.

As with all programs it is imperative that the standards are clear and followed. Ambiguity must be removed. For example, setting clear guidelines on what behavior earns recognition and which does not *is very important.*

Caution

Setting up contests that "reward" for quantity of improvements can cause people to spend an inordinate amount of time doing the things that help them win the contest. You get what you reward. This can also cause tension in the department, as the one pushing to win the contest may be seen as not contributing to his/her regular duties. Generally speaking, we do not recommend contests that reward one individual for doing the "most" or being the "best." This destroys teamwork, as individuals keep their good ideas to themselves so that they can win over the others. You want teamwork and sharing of good ideas. Therefore, group rewards for group achievements usually work better, and without the unintended consequences mentioned above. For example: "When the entire team sustains 95% 5S standards followed for 6 out of 8 weeks, everyone on the team earns a 5S Sustainers t-shirt."

Step 6: Demonstrate communication and recognition skills to the supervisors in your group. Be a leader. Ask them to go with you during your 5S Audit walks. Be sure to be empathetic during your discussions with the team. Gradually let

LESSONS FROM THE FIELD

As a "bad" example, we developed a contest whereby the department member got a letter to spell the company name every time they made an improvement. They had to show the improvement to the manager who then kept track on a public whiteboard. One employee made enough improvements in a week to easily win, blowing away the rest of the group. This actually upset the rest of the team as they felt the individual dropped his regular responsibilities, which then fell onto others. This imparted a negative tone with the program. So, instead of celebrating the victor and his improvements, it caused him to be an outsider and diminished future involvement from him and others.

them score the audit and say positive things to your team members for their adherence to 5S standards. In this way, you can coach them gradually in the skills that will help you *and* them to Sustain your 5S standards.

Tip

For training resources for sustaining 5S, including Michael McCarthy's *Sustain Your Gains* training delivered via the Internet to your plant conference room, contact Mike McCarthy at: mikemccarthy@sustainleangains.com. Also, to learn about improving communications skills, Scott Gauvin has a fantastic 3-day course on "People Centric Leadership," for more information contact the author at: David.Visco@the5Sstore.com.

Sustain: Summary of Steps

- ☐ Team signing of a 5S banner.
- ☐ Implement some visual management reminders.
- ☐ Develop 5S status communication methods.
- ☐ Create a 5S Communication Board.
- ☐ Develop a Rewards and Recognition program.
- ☐ Lead by example.

Action Items

1. _____
2. _____
3. _____
4. _____
5. _____
6. _____

Parking Lot Items

Ideas and issues out of scope but still worth capturing:

1. _____
2. _____
3. _____
4. _____
5. _____
6. _____

Chapter 9

The Ideal Conditions to Implement Lean

One of the most staggering statistics related to Lean implementation is its extremely low success rate: Nearly 98% of implementations fail. As such, I asked Scott Gauvin, president of Macresco, to provide additional insights into how you can succeed with your Lean implementation.

This is not because Lean methodology is not sound but rather, too often its application does not consider enough of the human element of the equation. Implementing Lean often entails big change—even when you implement on a modest scale. Add in some unwilling and skeptical participants and this change can create stress, which in turn leads to resistance, then apathy, and eventually, your project becomes part of the 98%.

To ensure Lean success and more importantly, sustain it, consider the following prerequisites to implementation:

Know What Your End Goal Is

Of all the Lean techniques, organizations tend to approach 5S with the most gusto. And it is no wonder—5S is an easy, low cost, simple to explain and understand foray into Lean. It is also applicable to a variety of functions and there is often a very visible impact to the area in which it was applied. So it feels easy to jump right into implementation without much organizational groundwork, and for the most part, it is.

A lack of preparation, however, is exactly why 5S is often about as sustainable as keeping your garage clean: Great for 2 weeks, but eventually you end up back where you started.

Before taking on 5S, you should know why you are doing it. *Hint*: Short-term cleanup should not be the goal. (Remember the garage?) And, though you may begin with departmentally related goals, they will not be sustainable without organization-wide support and longer-term vision.

Make Sure Leadership Is Onboard

Speaking of organization-wide support and long-term vision, having leadership onboard can often mean the difference between a siloed, short-term project and an effort that makes a meaningful impact on productivity and customer value.

Connecting with leadership is essential to ensuring that the implementation does not lose steam before it has had an impact. Sure, endorsement is helpful in the way of funding. But more importantly, leadership is understanding of Lean philosophy; its benefits beyond 5S and the purpose of this journey will help to smooth things over when you hit the cultural snags this change initiative will invariably hit.

Enlisting support before your program begins also gives you the opportunity to anchor your effort in the organization's purpose as well. In this way, you give leadership a genuine reason to support your program and ensure its future.

Prepare Your People

Unfortunately, well-intentioned but poorly conceived Lean programs have made people leery of continuous improvement—particularly if the programs have been attempted at the company before.

So, even if you are beginning with a small pilot, be transparent about your intentions with as large an audience as is possible—not just those that will be immediately involved. This will help to quell any anxiety that your participants or other employees may have about the program. Giving those involved a fair amount of notice will also allow them to process whatever doubts or concerns they have.

Do Not Lose Momentum

As I mentioned earlier, 5S is a great introduction to Lean. Though challenging at times, the process will likely create supporters and attract attention. Do not squander your hard-won success with inaction.

5S is a cyclical process as is continuous improvement so plan at the outset to manage sustainability, as it will require time and dedication to achieve. But most importantly, remember that 5S is just the first step in your Lean journey.

Thank you to Scott Gauvin from Macresco for this chapter. Read more about Gauvin in the "Acknowledgments" section at the end of the book.

Action Items

1. _____
2. _____
3. _____
4. _____

Parking Lot Items

Ideas and issues out of scope but still worth capturing:

1. _____
2. _____
3. _____
4. _____

In Closing

In closing, much has been made about how difficult 5S is to implement and sustain. I believe 5S success is attainable if you just follow the steps provided in this workbook and maintain momentum and vigilance. Once the initial training and implementation is in place, 5S is relatively straightforward if you just stay on course by not allowing complacency to settle in simply because you or your team is too busy. You will succeed if you stay on course, maintain your audits, keep your 5S materials stocked, recognize accomplishments, course correct where necessary, hold people accountable, and celebrate the successes.

Please make sure to contact me and let me know how your 5S program is going and if you need any help. I look forward to hearing from you. Best of luck.

David Visco
5S Expert
David.Visco@the5Sstore.com

5S Launch Guide

Develop Your Plan: Summary of Steps

☐ Get a 2-inch three-ring binder to store all of the project documents.
☐ Determine which area to implement 5S.
☐ Complete the Project Charter.
☐ Make a list of the tools and supplies you need.
☐ Inform all other departments about your implementation plan.
☐ Take plenty of *before* pictures.

Train the Team: Summary of Steps

☐ Use the *What*, *Why*, *Where*, *When*, and *How* format to explain what it is all about.
☐ Go through the PowerPoint presentation.
☐ Watch the 5S video.
☐ Play the 5S Nuts & Bolts Game.
☐ Conduct a Q&A session with the team.
☐ Capture team ideas.

Sort: Summary of Steps

☐ Write in the names of the people that attended the event.
☐ Review the benefits of Sort with the team.
☐ Quick review of how to fill out a 5S red tag properly.
☐ Start the red tag event.
☐ Take *after* photos of the area as well as the new red tag area.
☐ Discuss lessons learned with the team.
☐ Post your "before and after" document on your 5S Communication Board.

Set in Order: Summary of Steps

☐ Create your current state spaghetti diagram.
☐ Stand in a Circle Exercise.
☐ Discuss flow challenges with the team.
☐ Determine how and where to lay out your tools and equipment and get this step done.
☐ Conduct Shine while setting everything in order.
☐ Store unused 5S materials in the designated cabinet, shelf, room, and so on.
☐ Take *after* pictures and post them.
☐ Team discussion.

Standardize: Summary of Steps

☐ Develop your 5S Shine Map.
☐ Break your 5S Shine Map into quadrants and assign each team member.
☐ Discuss and develop a 5S Maintenance Chart.
☐ Discuss the 5S Audit program including the benefits along with a review of the Audit form and scoring.
☐ Conduct a 5S Audit.
☐ Review the results of the audit with the team and discuss scoring.
☐ Enter the scores into the 5S Audit Score Graph.
☐ Post the graph on the 5S Success whiteboard.

Sustain: Summary of Steps

☐ Team signing of a 5S banner.
☐ Implement some visual management reminders.
☐ Develop 5S status communication methods.
☐ Create a 5S Communication Board.
☐ Develop a Rewards and Recognition program.
☐ Lead by example.

5S Materials Checklist

All of the items in the checklist can be sourced from The 5S Store at: www. the5Sstore.com. One suggestion is to order one of the *5S Made Easy* Starter Kits.

5S Materials Checklist

Suggested Quantity	Items
1	5S *Fundamental* Principles of 5S Video
1	5S Nuts & Bolts Game
1	2" Vinyl Tape—Yellow, Green, Red, Blue, Black/Yellow, Black/White, Red/White
1	1" Vinyl Tape—Yellow, Green, Red, Blue, White, Black
20	Pallet Corner Markers
1	Pack of Red Tags
1	Red Tag Area Sign
TBD	5S Message Pens (One for each team member)
1	5S Poster
1	7 Wastes Poster
1	Roll of Tool Shadow Tape
1	Pegboard Kit
1	DIY Tool Foam Kit
1	Pack of 1 x 4 Dry Erase Magnets (white)
3	Gauge Marking Labels—One Green, Yellow, and Red
	Copies of *5S Made Easy* (1 book for each team member)

Forms

All forms can be downloaded from The 5S Store at: www.the5Sstore/5SMadeEasy.

- Form 1 shows the 5S Project Charter
- Form 2 shows the 5S Team Weekly Meeting
- Form 3 shows the 5S Audit Checklist
- Form 4 shows the 5S Visual Standards
- Form 5 shows the 5S Maintenance Chart

5S Project Charter

Project Authorization

Organization:		Coach:		Project Lead:	
Project Title:				Project Area Name:	

What are the challenges?

Project Objective:

Target Completion Date:		Estimated Benefits:	
Coach Signature:		Project Lead Signature:		Approval Date:	

Project Team

Name	Role	E-mail Address	Phone

Scope

Critical to Customer Satisfaction:

Inside Scope of Project	Outside Scope of Project

rev1

Form 1   5S Project Charter

5S Team Weekly Meeting   Week of _____   Dept _____   Shift _____

Team Members: _____

Achievements (list things that the team or team members did well with regard to 5S)

Areas to Improve

Who	Due Date

Audit Scores

Goal	Current	Previous Scores	# of Weeks We Sustained Goal
___	___	___ — ___ — ___	

Follow-up from Last Meeting

Who	Completed?

5S Made Easy rev1 2015

Form 2   5S Team Weekly Meeting

5S Audit Checklist

Status	Rating Level	# of Non-Conformities
Poor	1	5 or More
Fair	2	3–4
Good	3	2
Very Good	4	1
Best Practice	5	None

Audit Date:

Auditor(S):

Area:

Category		Score	Comments/Observations
Sort	**Objective: Determine What Is and Isn't Needed**	0	
	No unneeded equipment, tools, paperwork, etc., are present in area		
	All necessary items are clearly labeled		
	No unneeded inventory, supplies, parts, or materials (WIP) present in area		
	Personal items are not cluttering work area: tripping dangers are removed		
	Red Tag system is in place and unecessary items are tagged and stored		
Set in Order	**Objective: A Place for Everything and Everything in Its Place**	0	
	Designated areas are visually identified for finished, WIP, and pending jobs		
	Tools are at point of use and storage is visual (easy to see, retrieve, return)		
	Aisles, work areas, benches, equipment are clearly and consistently marked		
	Storage is above knees and below shoulders: work is at correct height		
	Paperwork and documents are properly organized and labeled		
Shine	**Objective: Clean to Inspection**	0	
	Floors, walls, stairs, surfaces, equipment are free of dirt, oil, grime and clutter		
	A maintenance system is in place to ensure periodic equipment inspection		
	Cleaning materials are well organized and easily accessible		
	Area is well lit and ventilated, labels and signs are legible/in good condition:		
	Shine responsibilities are clear and monitored regularly		
Standardize	**Objective: Standards to Keep the First 3 S's from Deteriorating**	0	
	5S Maintenance Schedule and Checklist are posted in the area		
	5S Visual Color Standards are posted and followed		
	Standard Work Instructions are posted		
	5S and continuous improvement results are posted and clear		
	Processes exist to monitor previous Audit Action items		
Sustain	**Objective: Make It a Habit**	0	
	5S Audits are conducted regularly		
	Supervisors are actively involved in 5S activities		
	Management conducts regularly scheduled gemba walks		
	All employees are trained in 5S and engaged to maintain the 5S Standard		
	Communication Boards are up to date		
	Total Score (of the above 25 boxes)	0	

Form 3   5S Audit Checklist (Courtesy of GBMP, Newton, MA.)

5S Visual Standards

Color Standard	Category	Description
Red	Hold/Quarantine	Rejects/Hold/Issues
Yellow	Warehouse Materials	Outgoing/Incoming Materials/Palletizing Areas
Green	Signals/Triggers	Kanban Locations
Blue	Tools & Accessories	Trash Cans, Pallet Jacks
Black/Yellow	Safety/Caution	Fire, PPE, Doorways
Black/White	Electrical	Electric Panels

Form 4   5S Visual Standards

5S Maintenance Chart

Area/Equipment Name:

Equipment No:

Authorized:

Frequency	Daily Maintenance	Weekly Maintenance	Monthly Maintenance	Quarterly Maintenance	Bi-Annual Maintenance	Annual Maintenance
Type of Maintenance	Adjustment	Inspection	Vacuum/Sweep/Dust	Lubrication	Clean/Scrub	

		January				February				March				April				May				June			
Activity	Description of Activity/Material Used	Owner	Daily	1/2/2015	1/9/2015	1/16/2015	1/23/2015	1/30/2015	2/6/2015	2/13/2015	2/20/2015	2/27/2015	3/6/2015	3/13/2015	3/20/2015	3/27/2015	4/3/2015	4/10/2015	4/17/2015	4/24/2015	5/1/2015	5/8/2015	5/15/2015	5/22/2015	5/29/2015	6/5/2015	6/12/2015	6/19/2015	6/26/2015
				1	2	3	4	5	6	7	8	9	10	11	12	13	14	15	16	17	18	19	20	21	22	23	24	25	26

Form 5   5S Maintenance Chart

Resources

Training and Education

Association of Manufacturing Excellence
www.ame.org

5S Best Practices
www.5SBestPractices.com

5S Virtual Coach
www.5SVirtualCoach.com

Scott Gauvin
scott.gauvin@macresco.com
www.macresco.com

GBMP
www.gbmp.org

Mike McCarthy
Author: *Sustain Your Gains—The People Side of Lean–Six Sigma*
Sustain Training via the Internet, delivered to your plant conference room
mikemccarthy@SustainLeanGains.com
www.SustainLeanGains.com

David Visco
Author: *5S Made Easy*
david.visco@the5Sstore.com

Supplies

The 5S Store
www.the5Sstore.com

Acknowledgments

I would like to thank a few of The 5S Store vendors/partners/customers that allowed us to use images of some of their solutions which we provide on our website. In no particular order, thank you to:

Accuform Signs	Lean Posters
Aerodyne Alloys	Macresco
Collins Bus Corporation	Kevin Meyer
Enna Products	Southwest Cheese
Ergomat	TREMCO
Fuss & O'Neill	Triton Products
GBMP	VIP Group
Hexion	TheVisualMachine.com
Inland Packaging	Western State Envelope & Label

A special thanks to Mike McCarthy from Sustain Lean Gains. He was my copy editor and provided me support and suggestions throughout the writing of this book. He also provided content for Chapter 8, "Sustain." He is the author of *Sustain Your Gains—The People Side of Lean–Six Sigma*. It is the best book I have read on the challenging subject of sustaining Lean improvements. McCarthy is available for webinars or on-site workshops. He can be contacted at: mikemccarthy@sustainleangains.com. His book can be found at The 5S Store.

A special thanks to Scott Gauvin, president of Macresco, an operations excellence consulting firm. He provided the content for Chapter 9: "The Ideal Conditions to Implement Lean." Gauvin is a seasoned change agent with more than 22 years experience successfully helping organizations realize their potential. Throughout his career, Gauvin's focus has been on driving performance gains through organizational alignment and a progressive approach to operations strategy. He has advised companies the world over and across a wide range of industries including pharmaceuticals, biotech, consumer goods, medical devices, agriculture, packaging, and industrial manufacturing. In addition to driving the growth of Macresco's consultancy practice, Gauvin counsels client organizations in transition and is most often involved in strategic endeavors that include assessing a company's capabilities and capacity for change as well as innovating underperforming business models to drive revenue and increase market opportunity. He holds a BA from the University of Massachusetts, an MBA from Boston University, and is a Six Sigma Black Belt. Scott Gauvin can be reached at: scott.gauvin@macresco.com.

Throughout my career there have been many people that have helped along the way in one way or another, either by direct support or simply believing in me. In no particular order I would like to thank each and every one of them here. Laura and Brian Visco, Eileen Carlson-Kelly, Karen Allen, Darren Hardy, Pat Wardwell, Chris Martin, Babson College, Mike Healey from Yeoman Technologies, Bob Chalmers, Robert Murphy, and of course The 5S Store team.

And, a final thank you to my partner, wife, and mother of our children, Barbara Visco. You have always been there to support me and listen to ideas. When I called you during my work lunch, that day 9 years ago after learning about 5S, saying I had an idea for a new business (which soon became The 5S Store), you said "Sounds good to me." I came home that evening to find you on our lone computer in our kitchen trying to figure out how to build an online store. It has been a heck of a ride ever since and I cannot wait to see what the future brings. I love you.

About the Author

David Visco is an experienced 5S coach and 5S event leader. He has 30 years of operations, warehousing, inventory management, and manufacturing experience in the distribution, medical device, biopharmaceutical, and the electronics industries. Visco has a master's degree from Babson College in Wellesley, Massachusetts. He lives with his wife and two children in Pepperell, Massachusetts. He also volunteers with the Association of Manufacturing Excellence (AME).

In 2006, after implementing 5S with his employer at the time, Visco had an idea to make 5S easier: one-stop shopping for 5S supplies and materials. He and his wife Barbara started *the5Sstore. com*, where you can get everything you need to implement 5S. Visco offers 5S advice to major corporations as well as small- and medium-sized companies. He also researches and finds visual solutions for applying 5S in difficult situations. If you are looking for ideas and solutions to your problems, or if you have questions, or if you simply want to know how to get started with 5S, contact David Visco at: david.visco@the5Sstore.com.

Index